50 Home Cooking Bible Recipes

By: Kelly Johnson

Table of Contents

- Classic Roast Chicken
- Beef Stew with Root Vegetables
- Homemade Meatloaf
- Creamy Mashed Potatoes
- Baked Mac and Cheese
- Chicken Pot Pie
- Slow-Cooked Pulled Pork
- Spaghetti Bolognese
- Roasted Vegetable Medley
- Classic Meatballs in Marinara Sauce
- Chicken Alfredo Pasta
- Beef Tacos with Fresh Salsa
- Shepherd's Pie
- Grilled BBQ Ribs
- Oven-Baked Fried Chicken
- Homemade Chicken Soup
- Macaroni and Cheese with Bacon

- Grilled Cheese and Tomato Soup
- Lasagna with Ricotta and Spinach
- Shrimp Scampi Pasta
- Beef and Broccoli Stir-Fry
- Chicken Parmesan
- Pork Chops with Apple Sauce
- Classic Caesar Salad
- Beef Wellington
- Braised Short Ribs
- Clam Chowder
- Chili with Ground Beef and Beans
- Roast Beef with Horseradish Sauce
- Baked Salmon with Lemon and Dill
- Chicken and Dumplings
- Stuffed Bell Peppers
- Roast Pork Loin with Garlic and Rosemary
- Grilled Steaks with Herb Butter
- Stir-Fried Veggies with Tofu
- Eggplant Parmesan

- Sweet and Sour Chicken
- Lemon Garlic Roasted Chicken
- Beef Fajitas
- Cornbread with Honey Butter
- Baked Ziti with Italian Sausage
- Beef Brisket
- Broccoli Cheddar Soup
- Chicken and Rice Casserole
- Sausage and Peppers
- Pot Roast with Carrots and Potatoes
- Creamy Shrimp and Grits
- Sautéed Garlic Spinach
- Roasted Brussels Sprouts with Bacon
- Sweet Potato Casserole

Classic Roast Chicken

- Ingredients:

    1. 1 whole chicken (3-4 lbs)
    2. 2 tbsp olive oil
    3. 1 lemon, halved
    4. 4 cloves garlic, smashed
    5. 1 onion, quartered
    6. Fresh herbs (rosemary, thyme, or parsley)
    7. Salt and pepper to taste

- Instructions:

    1. Preheat the oven to 425°F (220°C).
    2. Pat the chicken dry with paper towels and rub it with olive oil, salt, and pepper.
    3. Stuff the chicken cavity with lemon halves, garlic, onion, and herbs.
    4. Tie the legs with kitchen twine and tuck the wings under the body.
    5. Place the chicken on a roasting rack in a roasting pan and roast for 1 hour 15 minutes to 1 hour 30 minutes, or until the internal temperature reaches 165°F (74°C).
    6. Let the chicken rest for 10 minutes before carving.

Beef Stew with Root Vegetables

- Ingredients:

    1. 2 lbs beef stew meat, cubed
    2. 1 tbsp olive oil
    3. 1 onion, chopped
    4. 3 cloves garlic, minced
    5. 4 cups beef broth
    6. 4 large carrots, peeled and sliced
    7. 3 medium potatoes, peeled and cubed
    8. 2 parsnips, peeled and sliced
    9. 2 bay leaves
    10. Salt and pepper to taste
    11. Fresh thyme

- Instructions:

    1. In a large pot, heat olive oil over medium heat. Brown the beef in batches, then remove and set aside.
    2. In the same pot, sauté onion and garlic until softened.
    3. Return the beef to the pot and add beef broth, carrots, potatoes, parsnips, bay leaves, thyme, salt, and pepper.
    4. Bring to a boil, then reduce heat and simmer for 2 hours, or until the meat is tender and the vegetables are cooked through.

5. Serve hot, garnished with fresh thyme.

Homemade Meatloaf

- Ingredients:

    1. 1 lb ground beef
    2. 1/2 lb ground pork
    3. 1 onion, finely chopped
    4. 2 cloves garlic, minced
    5. 1/2 cup breadcrumbs
    6. 1/4 cup milk
    7. 1 large egg
    8. 1/4 cup ketchup
    9. 1 tbsp Worcestershire sauce
    10. Salt and pepper to taste
    11. 1/4 cup ketchup (for topping)

- Instructions:

    1. Preheat the oven to 375°F (190°C).
    2. In a large bowl, combine beef, pork, onion, garlic, breadcrumbs, milk, egg, ketchup, Worcestershire sauce, salt, and pepper.
    3. Shape the mixture into a loaf and place in a greased baking dish.
    4. Top with 1/4 cup ketchup.

5. Bake for 45-50 minutes, or until the meatloaf reaches an internal temperature of 160°F (71°C).

6. Let rest for 10 minutes before slicing.

Creamy Mashed Potatoes

- Ingredients:

    1. 2 lbs potatoes, peeled and chopped
    2. 1/2 cup butter
    3. 1/2 cup heavy cream
    4. Salt and pepper to taste
    5. Garlic (optional)

- Instructions:

    1. In a large pot, boil potatoes in salted water until tender, about 15-20 minutes.
    2. Drain the potatoes and return them to the pot.
    3. Add butter and cream, and mash until smooth.
    4. Season with salt and pepper, and add garlic for extra flavor if desired.

Baked Mac and Cheese

- Ingredients:

    1. 1 lb elbow macaroni
    2. 2 cups shredded sharp cheddar cheese
    3. 1/2 cup grated Parmesan cheese
    4. 2 cups milk
    5. 2 tbsp butter
    6. 2 tbsp all-purpose flour
    7. 1/2 tsp mustard powder
    8. Salt and pepper to taste
    9. 1/2 cup breadcrumbs (optional)

- Instructions:

    1. Preheat the oven to 350°F (175°C).
    2. Cook the macaroni according to package directions, then drain and set aside.
    3. In a saucepan, melt butter over medium heat. Add flour and whisk for 1-2 minutes.
    4. Gradually add milk, whisking constantly until the sauce thickens.
    5. Stir in cheddar and Parmesan cheeses, mustard powder, salt, and pepper until smooth.

6. Combine cooked macaroni with cheese sauce and pour into a greased baking dish.

7. Top with breadcrumbs, if using, and bake for 25-30 minutes, until golden and bubbly.

Chicken Pot Pie

- Ingredients:

    1. 2 cups cooked chicken, shredded
    2. 1 cup frozen peas and carrots
    3. 1/2 cup onion, chopped
    4. 1/4 cup butter
    5. 1/4 cup flour
    6. 2 cups chicken broth
    7. 1/2 cup heavy cream
    8. 1 tsp thyme
    9. Salt and pepper to taste
    10. 2 pre-made pie crusts

- Instructions:

    1. Preheat the oven to 400°F (200°C).
    2. In a saucepan, melt butter and sauté onion until softened.
    3. Add flour and cook for 1-2 minutes, then gradually whisk in chicken broth and heavy cream.
    4. Stir in thyme, salt, pepper, chicken, and vegetables. Simmer until the mixture thickens.
    5. Place one pie crust in a pie dish and fill with the chicken mixture.

6. Top with the second pie crust, sealing the edges and cutting a few slits in the top.

7. Bake for 30-35 minutes, until golden brown.

Slow-Cooked Pulled Pork

- Ingredients:
    1. 4 lbs pork shoulder
    2. 1 onion, sliced
    3. 1/2 cup BBQ sauce
    4. 1/4 cup apple cider vinegar
    5. 1/4 cup brown sugar
    6. 1 tbsp paprika
    7. 1 tsp garlic powder
    8. Salt and pepper to taste

- Instructions:
    1. Place the pork shoulder in a slow cooker and season with paprika, garlic powder, salt, and pepper.
    2. Top with onion, BBQ sauce, apple cider vinegar, and brown sugar.
    3. Cook on low for 8 hours or until the pork is tender and easily shredded.
    4. Shred the pork with two forks and stir it into the sauce. Serve on buns.

Spaghetti Bolognese

- Ingredients:

    1. 1 lb ground beef or pork
    2. 1 onion, chopped
    3. 2 cloves garlic, minced
    4. 1 can (28 oz) crushed tomatoes
    5. 1/4 cup red wine (optional)
    6. 1 tsp dried oregano
    7. Salt and pepper to taste
    8. 1 lb spaghetti

- Instructions:

    1. In a large pan, brown the ground meat over medium heat.
    2. Add onion and garlic, cooking until softened.
    3. Stir in crushed tomatoes, red wine (if using), oregano, salt, and pepper. Simmer for 30 minutes.
    4. Meanwhile, cook spaghetti according to package directions.
    5. Serve the sauce over pasta, garnished with Parmesan cheese.

Roasted Vegetable Medley

- Ingredients:

    1. 2 cups broccoli florets
    2. 2 carrots, sliced
    3. 1 bell pepper, chopped
    4. 1 zucchini, sliced
    5. 2 tbsp olive oil
    6. Salt and pepper to taste
    7. Fresh herbs (rosemary, thyme)

- Instructions:

    1. Preheat the oven to 400°F (200°C).
    2. Toss the vegetables with olive oil, salt, pepper, and herbs.
    3. Spread them in a single layer on a baking sheet and roast for 25-30 minutes, stirring halfway through, until tender.

Classic Meatballs in Marinara Sauce

- Ingredients:

    1. 1 lb ground beef or a mix of beef and pork
    2. 1/2 cup breadcrumbs
    3. 1/4 cup grated Parmesan cheese
    4. 1 egg
    5. 1/4 cup milk
    6. 2 cloves garlic, minced
    7. 2 cups marinara sauce
    8. Salt and pepper to taste

- Instructions:

    1. Preheat the oven to 375°F (190°C).
    2. In a bowl, mix the meat, breadcrumbs, Parmesan, egg, milk, garlic, salt, and pepper.
    3. Form into meatballs and place on a baking sheet.
    4. Bake for 15-20 minutes, until browned.
    5. While the meatballs bake, simmer the marinara sauce in a large pan.
    6. Add the cooked meatballs to the sauce and cook for 10 minutes. Serve with spaghetti or bread.

Chicken Alfredo Pasta

- Ingredients:

    1. 2 chicken breasts, boneless and skinless

    2. 1 tbsp olive oil

    3. Salt and pepper to taste

    4. 12 oz fettuccine pasta

    5. 2 tbsp butter

    6. 3 cloves garlic, minced

    7. 1 cup heavy cream

    8. 1 cup grated Parmesan cheese

    9. Fresh parsley, chopped (for garnish)

- Instructions:

    1. Cook fettuccine pasta according to package directions, then drain and set aside.

    2. Season chicken breasts with salt and pepper. Heat olive oil in a pan over medium heat and cook the chicken for 6-7 minutes per side until fully cooked. Let rest before slicing.

    3. In the same pan, melt butter and sauté garlic for 1 minute until fragrant.

    4. Stir in heavy cream and simmer for 2-3 minutes.

    5. Add Parmesan cheese, stirring until the sauce thickens. Season with salt and pepper.

6. Toss the pasta in the Alfredo sauce and top with sliced chicken. Garnish with fresh parsley.

Beef Tacos with Fresh Salsa

- Ingredients:

    1. 1 lb ground beef
    2. 1 packet taco seasoning or homemade seasoning
    3. 8 soft or hard taco shells
    4. 1 cup shredded lettuce
    5. 1 cup diced tomatoes
    6. 1/4 cup diced red onion
    7. 1/4 cup chopped cilantro
    8. 1 lime, cut into wedges
    9. 1/2 cup sour cream (optional)
    10. Salsa (for topping)

- Instructions:

    1. Cook ground beef in a pan over medium heat until browned, breaking it apart as it cooks. Drain excess fat.
    2. Stir in taco seasoning and follow the instructions on the packet, or add your own seasoning mix and water to taste. Simmer for a few minutes.
    3. Heat taco shells according to package instructions.
    4. Assemble tacos by filling each shell with seasoned beef, shredded lettuce, tomatoes, onions, cilantro, and a squeeze of lime juice. Top with salsa and sour cream.

Shepherd's Pie

- Ingredients:

    1. 1 lb ground lamb (or beef for cottage pie)
    2. 1 onion, chopped
    3. 2 carrots, diced
    4. 2 cloves garlic, minced
    5. 1 cup frozen peas
    6. 1/4 cup beef broth
    7. 2 tbsp tomato paste
    8. 1 tsp dried thyme
    9. Salt and pepper to taste
    10. 4 cups mashed potatoes (prepared)
    11. 1/4 cup grated cheddar cheese (optional)

- Instructions:

    1. Preheat the oven to 375°F (190°C).
    2. Brown the ground lamb in a large skillet over medium heat. Drain excess fat.
    3. Add onions, carrots, and garlic. Cook until softened, about 5-7 minutes.
    4. Stir in peas, tomato paste, beef broth, thyme, salt, and pepper. Simmer for 10 minutes, then remove from heat.

5. Spread the meat mixture into a baking dish and top with mashed potatoes.

6. Sprinkle with cheese, if using, and bake for 25-30 minutes until golden and bubbly.

Grilled BBQ Ribs

- Ingredients:

    1. 2 racks of baby back ribs
    2. 1/4 cup olive oil
    3. 1/4 cup brown sugar
    4. 1/4 cup paprika
    5. 1 tbsp salt
    6. 1 tbsp black pepper
    7. 1 tbsp garlic powder
    8. 1/2 cup BBQ sauce (for glazing)

- Instructions:

    1. Preheat the grill to medium heat.
    2. Mix olive oil, brown sugar, paprika, salt, pepper, and garlic powder in a bowl.
    3. Rub the spice mixture all over the ribs.
    4. Grill ribs for 1.5-2 hours, turning occasionally, until tender.
    5. During the last 10 minutes of grilling, brush with BBQ sauce and cook for additional caramelization.
    6. Remove from grill, rest for 5 minutes, then slice and serve.

Oven-Baked Fried Chicken

- Ingredients:

    1. 4 chicken pieces (legs, thighs, breasts)
    2. 1 cup buttermilk
    3. 1 cup all-purpose flour
    4. 1 tsp paprika
    5. 1 tsp garlic powder
    6. 1/2 tsp salt
    7. 1/2 tsp black pepper
    8. 2 tbsp vegetable oil

- Instructions:

    1. Preheat the oven to 400°F (200°C) and line a baking sheet with parchment paper.
    2. Soak chicken pieces in buttermilk for at least 1 hour.
    3. In a bowl, mix flour, paprika, garlic powder, salt, and pepper.
    4. Dredge the soaked chicken in the seasoned flour mixture, ensuring even coating.
    5. Place chicken on the baking sheet and drizzle with vegetable oil.
    6. Bake for 35-40 minutes, or until the chicken is golden and cooked through.

Homemade Chicken Soup

- Ingredients:

    1. 2 chicken breasts or thighs
    2. 1 onion, chopped
    3. 2 carrots, diced
    4. 2 celery stalks, diced
    5. 4 cups chicken broth
    6. 2 cloves garlic, minced
    7. 1 bay leaf
    8. Salt and pepper to taste
    9. 1 cup egg noodles or rice

- Instructions:

    1. In a large pot, cook chicken with onion, carrots, and celery until the chicken is cooked through, about 20-25 minutes.
    2. Remove the chicken, shred it, and return it to the pot.
    3. Add chicken broth, garlic, bay leaf, salt, and pepper, and bring to a boil.
    4. Add egg noodles or rice and cook until tender, about 10-12 minutes.
    5. Taste for seasoning and serve warm.

Macaroni and Cheese with Bacon

- Ingredients:

    1. 12 oz elbow macaroni
    2. 4 slices bacon, cooked and crumbled
    3. 2 tbsp butter
    4. 2 tbsp flour
    5. 2 cups milk
    6. 2 cups shredded cheddar cheese
    7. Salt and pepper to taste

- Instructions:

    1. Cook macaroni according to package instructions and set aside.
    2. In a saucepan, melt butter and whisk in flour. Cook for 1-2 minutes.
    3. Gradually add milk while whisking, then simmer until thickened.
    4. Stir in cheese until melted and smooth. Season with salt and pepper.
    5. Toss the cooked macaroni with the cheese sauce and crumbled bacon. Serve hot.

Grilled Cheese and Tomato Soup

- Ingredients:

    1. 2 slices bread

    2. 2 slices cheddar cheese

    3. 1 tbsp butter

    4. 1 can (14 oz) tomato soup

    5. 1/2 tsp garlic powder

    6. Salt and pepper to taste

- Instructions:

    1. Heat tomato soup in a pot over medium heat. Add garlic powder, salt, and pepper, and simmer until warm.

    2. Butter the bread slices and place cheese in between.

    3. Grill the sandwich in a skillet over medium heat for 2-3 minutes on each side until golden brown and the cheese is melted.

    4. Serve the grilled cheese sandwich alongside the tomato soup.

Lasagna with Ricotta and Spinach

- Ingredients:

    1. 12 lasagna noodles
    2. 1 lb ricotta cheese
    3. 1 1/2 cups cooked spinach, drained
    4. 2 cups marinara sauce
    5. 2 cups shredded mozzarella cheese
    6. 1/2 cup grated Parmesan cheese
    7. 1 egg

- Instructions:

    1. Preheat the oven to 375°F (190°C).
    2. Cook lasagna noodles according to package instructions, then drain and set aside.
    3. In a bowl, mix ricotta cheese, cooked spinach, egg, and Parmesan cheese.
    4. Spread a layer of marinara sauce in a baking dish, then layer with noodles, ricotta mixture, mozzarella, and sauce.
    5. Repeat layers until ingredients are used, ending with mozzarella and sauce on top.
    6. Cover with foil and bake for 30 minutes. Remove foil and bake for an additional 10-15 minutes until bubbly and golden.

Shrimp Scampi Pasta

- Ingredients:

    1. 1 lb shrimp, peeled and deveined
    2. 12 oz spaghetti or linguine
    3. 4 tbsp butter
    4. 4 cloves garlic, minced
    5. 1/4 cup white wine (optional)
    6. 1 tbsp lemon juice
    7. Fresh parsley, chopped
    8. Salt and pepper to taste

- Instructions:

    1. Cook pasta according to package directions and set aside.
    2. In a large skillet, melt butter and sauté garlic until fragrant.
    3. Add shrimp to the pan and cook for 2-3 minutes per side until pink.
    4. Add white wine (if using) and lemon juice, simmer for 2 minutes.
    5. Toss pasta with the shrimp and sauce, then garnish with fresh parsley and serve.

Beef and Broccoli Stir-Fry

- Ingredients:

    1. 1 lb beef sirloin, thinly sliced
    2. 3 cups broccoli florets
    3. 2 tbsp soy sauce
    4. 1 tbsp oyster sauce
    5. 1 tbsp hoisin sauce
    6. 1 tbsp cornstarch
    7. 2 tbsp vegetable oil
    8. 2 cloves garlic, minced
    9. 1 tsp ginger, grated
    10. 1/4 cup beef broth
    11. Salt and pepper to taste

- Instructions:

    1. In a bowl, mix soy sauce, oyster sauce, hoisin sauce, cornstarch, and beef broth to make the stir-fry sauce.
    2. Heat vegetable oil in a wok or large skillet over medium-high heat. Add beef and cook for 2-3 minutes until browned.
    3. Remove the beef and set aside. In the same pan, add garlic and ginger and sauté for 1 minute.
    4. Add broccoli and stir-fry for 4-5 minutes until tender-crisp.

5. Add the beef back into the pan and pour the sauce over. Stir to coat and cook for 1-2 minutes until the sauce thickens.

6. Serve with steamed rice or noodles.

Chicken Parmesan

- Ingredients:

    1. 4 boneless, skinless chicken breasts
    2. 1 cup flour
    3. 2 eggs, beaten
    4. 1 1/2 cups breadcrumbs
    5. 1/2 cup grated Parmesan cheese
    6. 2 cups marinara sauce
    7. 1 1/2 cups shredded mozzarella cheese
    8. 1/4 cup fresh basil, chopped
    9. Olive oil for frying

- Instructions:

    1. Preheat the oven to 375°F (190°C).
    2. Dredge chicken breasts in flour, dip in beaten eggs, then coat with a mixture of breadcrumbs and Parmesan cheese.
    3. Heat olive oil in a large skillet over medium heat and fry the chicken for 3-4 minutes per side until golden and crispy.
    4. Place the fried chicken in a baking dish and top each piece with marinara sauce and mozzarella cheese.
    5. Bake for 20-25 minutes until the cheese is melted and bubbly. Garnish with fresh basil.

Pork Chops with Apple Sauce

- Ingredients:

    1. 4 bone-in pork chops

    2. Salt and pepper to taste

    3. 2 tbsp olive oil

    4. 1 cup applesauce

    5. 1/2 tsp cinnamon

    6. 1 tbsp honey (optional)

- Instructions:

    1. Season the pork chops with salt and pepper on both sides.

    2. Heat olive oil in a skillet over medium-high heat and cook the pork chops for 4-5 minutes per side until golden brown and cooked through.

    3. In a separate saucepan, heat applesauce with cinnamon and honey (if using) over low heat. Stir occasionally.

    4. Serve the pork chops with a spoonful of warm apple sauce on top.

Classic Caesar Salad

- Ingredients:

    1. 4 cups Romaine lettuce, chopped
    2. 1/2 cup Caesar dressing
    3. 1/4 cup grated Parmesan cheese
    4. Croutons
    5. Freshly ground black pepper

- Instructions:

    1. In a large bowl, toss the Romaine lettuce with Caesar dressing until well coated.
    2. Add grated Parmesan cheese and toss again.
    3. Top with croutons and freshly ground black pepper before serving.

Beef Wellington

- Ingredients:

    1. 1 1/2 lb beef tenderloin, trimmed
    2. Salt and pepper to taste
    3. 2 tbsp olive oil
    4. 1/2 cup pâté or mushroom duxelles
    5. 1 package puff pastry
    6. 1 egg, beaten (for egg wash)

- Instructions:

    1. Preheat the oven to 400°F (200°C).
    2. Season beef tenderloin with salt and pepper. Heat olive oil in a skillet over high heat and sear the beef on all sides for 3-4 minutes.
    3. Let the beef cool, then spread pâté or mushroom duxelles over the beef.
    4. Roll out the puff pastry and wrap the beef in it, sealing the edges. Brush the pastry with egg wash.
    5. Bake for 25-30 minutes, or until the pastry is golden brown and the beef is medium-rare. Let rest before slicing.

Braised Short Ribs

- Ingredients:

    1. 4-6 beef short ribs
    2. 2 tbsp olive oil
    3. Salt and pepper to taste
    4. 1 onion, chopped
    5. 2 carrots, chopped
    6. 2 celery stalks, chopped
    7. 2 cloves garlic, minced
    8. 1 cup red wine
    9. 2 cups beef broth
    10. 1 sprig thyme

- Instructions:

    1. Preheat the oven to 325°F (165°C).
    2. Season short ribs with salt and pepper. Heat olive oil in a large Dutch oven and sear the short ribs on all sides.
    3. Remove ribs and set aside. In the same pot, sauté onion, carrots, celery, and garlic until softened, about 5 minutes.
    4. Add red wine and scrape up any browned bits from the bottom. Stir in beef broth and thyme.

5. Return the short ribs to the pot, cover, and transfer to the oven. Braise for 2.5-3 hours, or until the meat is tender.

6. Serve with mashed potatoes or crusty bread.

Clam Chowder

- Ingredients:

    1. 2 tbsp butter
    2. 1 onion, chopped
    3. 2 celery stalks, chopped
    4. 2 medium potatoes, diced
    5. 1 lb clams, cleaned and chopped
    6. 3 cups clam juice
    7. 1 cup heavy cream
    8. 1/4 cup flour
    9. Salt and pepper to taste
    10. Fresh parsley, chopped

- Instructions:

    1. In a large pot, melt butter over medium heat. Add onion and celery, and sauté until softened.
    2. Add potatoes and clam juice, bringing to a boil. Reduce heat and simmer for 10-12 minutes until potatoes are tender.
    3. Stir in flour and cook for 2 minutes. Gradually add the heavy cream, stirring to thicken the soup.
    4. Add chopped clams and cook for 2-3 minutes until heated through. Season with salt and pepper.

5. Garnish with fresh parsley and serve with crusty bread.

Chili with Ground Beef and Beans

- Ingredients:

    1. 1 lb ground beef
    2. 1 onion, chopped
    3. 2 cloves garlic, minced
    4. 1 can (15 oz) kidney beans, drained and rinsed
    5. 1 can (15 oz) black beans, drained and rinsed
    6. 1 can (14.5 oz) diced tomatoes
    7. 2 tbsp chili powder
    8. 1 tsp cumin
    9. 1/2 tsp paprika
    10. Salt and pepper to taste

- Instructions:

    1. In a large pot, brown the ground beef over medium heat. Drain excess fat.
    2. Add onion and garlic and sauté until softened, about 5 minutes.
    3. Stir in beans, diced tomatoes, chili powder, cumin, paprika, salt, and pepper.
    4. Bring to a boil, then reduce heat and simmer for 30 minutes, stirring occasionally.
    5. Serve with sour cream, shredded cheese, and crackers.

Roast Beef with Horseradish Sauce

- Ingredients:

    1. 3 lb beef roast (such as ribeye or sirloin)
    2. Salt and pepper to taste
    3. 2 tbsp olive oil
    4. 1/4 cup prepared horseradish
    5. 1/2 cup sour cream
    6. 1 tbsp lemon juice

- Instructions:

    1. Preheat the oven to 375°F (190°C).
    2. Season the beef roast with salt and pepper. Heat olive oil in a skillet and sear the roast on all sides for 3-4 minutes.
    3. Transfer the roast to a baking dish and roast for 1-1.5 hours, or until desired doneness is reached.
    4. While the roast is cooking, mix horseradish, sour cream, and lemon juice in a bowl.
    5. Slice the roast and serve with the horseradish sauce.

Baked Salmon with Lemon and Dill

- Ingredients:

    1. 4 salmon fillets
    2. 2 tbsp olive oil
    3. Salt and pepper to taste
    4. 1 lemon, sliced
    5. 2 tbsp fresh dill, chopped

- Instructions:

    1. Preheat the oven to 375°F (190°C).
    2. Place salmon fillets on a baking sheet and drizzle with olive oil. Season with salt and pepper.
    3. Top each fillet with lemon slices and sprinkle with fresh dill.
    4. Bake for 12-15 minutes, or until the salmon is cooked through and flakes easily with a fork.
    5. Serve with steamed vegetables or rice.

Chicken and Dumplings

- Ingredients:

    1. 1 lb chicken breast or thighs, cooked and shredded
    2. 4 cups chicken broth
    3. 2 cups whole milk
    4. 1 onion, chopped
    5. 2 carrots, chopped
    6. 2 celery stalks, chopped
    7. 2 cloves garlic, minced
    8. 2 cups all-purpose flour
    9. 1 1/2 tsp baking powder
    10. 1/2 tsp salt
    11. 1/4 tsp pepper
    12. 1/4 cup butter
    13. 1/2 cup milk
    14. Fresh parsley, chopped (for garnish)

- Instructions:

    1. In a large pot, sauté onion, carrots, celery, and garlic in butter over medium heat for 5-7 minutes until softened.
    2. Add chicken broth and whole milk. Bring to a simmer.

3. In a separate bowl, mix flour, baking powder, salt, and pepper. Add 1/4 cup butter and 1/2 cup milk, mixing until a thick dough forms.

4. Drop spoonfuls of the dumpling dough into the simmering soup. Cover and cook for 10-12 minutes until dumplings are cooked through.

5. Add shredded chicken to the soup and stir to combine. Garnish with fresh parsley and serve.

Stuffed Bell Peppers

- Ingredients:

    1. 4 bell peppers, tops cut off and seeds removed
    2. 1 lb ground beef or turkey
    3. 1 cup cooked rice
    4. 1 onion, chopped
    5. 2 cloves garlic, minced
    6. 1 can (15 oz) tomato sauce
    7. 1 tsp Italian seasoning
    8. Salt and pepper to taste
    9. 1 cup shredded cheese (optional)

- Instructions:

    1. Preheat oven to 375°F (190°C).
    2. In a skillet, cook ground meat, onion, and garlic over medium heat until the meat is browned.
    3. Stir in tomato sauce, cooked rice, Italian seasoning, salt, and pepper. Simmer for 5 minutes.
    4. Stuff the bell peppers with the meat mixture and place them in a baking dish.
    5. Cover with foil and bake for 30 minutes. Remove the foil, top with cheese if desired, and bake for an additional 10-15 minutes until the peppers are tender.

Roast Pork Loin with Garlic and Rosemary

- Ingredients:

    1. 3 lb pork loin
    2. 4 cloves garlic, minced
    3. 2 tbsp fresh rosemary, chopped
    4. 2 tbsp olive oil
    5. Salt and pepper to taste
    6. 1 cup chicken broth

- Instructions:

    1. Preheat oven to 375°F (190°C).
    2. Rub the pork loin with olive oil, minced garlic, rosemary, salt, and pepper.
    3. Place the pork in a roasting pan and pour chicken broth around it.
    4. Roast for 1-1.5 hours, or until the internal temperature reaches 145°F (63°C). Let rest before slicing.

Grilled Steaks with Herb Butter

- Ingredients:

    1. 4 steaks (ribeye, sirloin, or your choice)
    2. Salt and pepper to taste
    3. 1/2 cup unsalted butter, softened
    4. 2 tbsp fresh parsley, chopped
    5. 1 tbsp fresh thyme, chopped
    6. 1 tsp garlic powder

- Instructions:

    1. Preheat grill to medium-high heat.
    2. Season steaks with salt and pepper.
    3. Grill steaks for 4-5 minutes per side for medium-rare (or cook to desired doneness).
    4. In a small bowl, mix softened butter with parsley, thyme, and garlic powder.
    5. Top each steak with a dollop of herb butter and serve.

Stir-Fried Veggies with Tofu

- Ingredients:

    1. 1 block firm tofu, drained and cubed
    2. 2 tbsp soy sauce
    3. 2 tbsp sesame oil
    4. 1 red bell pepper, sliced
    5. 1 zucchini, sliced
    6. 1 carrot, sliced
    7. 1 cup broccoli florets
    8. 2 cloves garlic, minced
    9. 1 tbsp fresh ginger, grated
    10. 2 tbsp green onions, chopped
    11. 1 tbsp sesame seeds (optional)

- Instructions:

    1. Press tofu to remove excess water, then cut into cubes.
    2. Heat 1 tablespoon of sesame oil in a wok or large skillet over medium heat. Add tofu and cook for 5-7 minutes until golden and crispy. Remove from the skillet.
    3. In the same skillet, add remaining sesame oil and sauté garlic, ginger, and vegetables for 5-7 minutes until tender-crisp.

4. Add tofu back into the skillet, pour in soy sauce, and toss to combine. Garnish with green onions and sesame seeds.

Eggplant Parmesan

- Ingredients:

    1. 2 medium eggplants, sliced into rounds
    2. Salt
    3. 1 1/2 cups breadcrumbs
    4. 1/2 cup grated Parmesan cheese
    5. 2 cups marinara sauce
    6. 1 1/2 cups shredded mozzarella cheese
    7. 1 egg, beaten
    8. Olive oil for frying

- Instructions:

    1. Sprinkle eggplant slices with salt and let sit for 30 minutes to remove excess moisture. Pat dry with paper towels.
    2. Preheat oven to 375°F (190°C). Dip eggplant slices in beaten egg, then coat with breadcrumbs and Parmesan cheese.
    3. Heat olive oil in a skillet over medium heat and fry eggplant slices until golden brown on both sides.
    4. In a baking dish, layer fried eggplant with marinara sauce and mozzarella cheese. Repeat layers until all eggplant is used.
    5. Bake for 20-25 minutes until the cheese is melted and bubbly.

Sweet and Sour Chicken

- Ingredients:

    1. 1 lb chicken breast, cubed
    2. 1/2 cup cornstarch
    3. 2 tbsp vegetable oil
    4. 1/2 cup bell pepper, chopped
    5. 1/2 cup onion, chopped
    6. 1/2 cup pineapple chunks
    7. 1/2 cup rice vinegar
    8. 1/4 cup ketchup
    9. 1/4 cup soy sauce
    10. 2 tbsp sugar
    11. 1 tbsp sesame oil

- Instructions:

    1. Coat chicken cubes in cornstarch.
    2. Heat vegetable oil in a skillet and cook chicken until golden and cooked through, about 5-7 minutes.
    3. Remove chicken and sauté bell pepper, onion, and pineapple for 2-3 minutes.
    4. In a small bowl, whisk together vinegar, ketchup, soy sauce, sugar, and sesame oil. Pour over the vegetables and bring to a simmer.

5. Add chicken back to the skillet and stir to coat. Serve with rice.

Lemon Garlic Roasted Chicken

- Ingredients:

    1. 1 whole chicken (about 4 lb)
    2. 4 cloves garlic, minced
    3. 1 lemon, halved
    4. 1/4 cup olive oil
    5. 1 tsp rosemary
    6. Salt and pepper to taste

- Instructions:

    1. Preheat oven to 425°F (220°C).
    2. Rub the chicken with olive oil, minced garlic, rosemary, salt, and pepper.
    3. Stuff the cavity with lemon halves.
    4. Roast for 1 hour and 15 minutes, or until the chicken reaches an internal temperature of 165°F (74°C). Let rest before carving.

Beef Fajitas

- Ingredients:
    1. 1 lb flank steak or skirt steak
    2. 1 onion, sliced
    3. 1 bell pepper, sliced
    4. 2 tbsp olive oil
    5. 2 tsp chili powder
    6. 1 tsp cumin
    7. 1 tsp paprika
    8. Salt and pepper to taste
    9. Flour tortillas
    10. Lime wedges, for serving

- Instructions:
    1. Preheat a grill or skillet over medium-high heat.
    2. Season steak with chili powder, cumin, paprika, salt, and pepper.
    3. Grill steak for 4-5 minutes per side for medium-rare. Let rest before slicing thinly.
    4. Sauté onions and bell peppers in olive oil until softened, about 5-7 minutes.
    5. Serve steak and veggies in flour tortillas with lime wedges.

Cornbread with Honey Butter

- Ingredients:

    1. 1 cup cornmeal
    2. 1 cup all-purpose flour
    3. 1/4 cup sugar
    4. 1 tbsp baking powder
    5. 1/2 tsp salt
    6. 1 cup buttermilk
    7. 1/2 cup melted butter
    8. 2 eggs
    9. 1/4 cup honey (for honey butter)
    10. 1/2 cup softened butter (for honey butter)

- Instructions:

    1. Preheat oven to 400°F (200°C). Grease a baking dish or cast-iron skillet.
    2. In a large bowl, whisk together cornmeal, flour, sugar, baking powder, and salt.
    3. Stir in buttermilk, melted butter, and eggs until combined.
    4. Pour the batter into the prepared dish and bake for 20-25 minutes, until golden and a toothpick comes out clean.
    5. In a small bowl, mix softened butter and honey to make the honey butter. Serve with cornbread.

Baked Ziti with Italian Sausage

- Ingredients:

    1. 1 lb ziti pasta
    2. 1 lb Italian sausage, removed from casing
    3. 2 cups marinara sauce
    4. 2 cups ricotta cheese
    5. 1 1/2 cups shredded mozzarella cheese
    6. 1/2 cup grated Parmesan cheese
    7. 1 egg
    8. 2 cloves garlic, minced
    9. 1 tsp dried basil
    10. 1 tsp dried oregano
    11. Salt and pepper to taste

- Instructions:

    1. Preheat oven to 375°F (190°C).
    2. Cook ziti according to package directions. Drain and set aside.
    3. In a skillet, cook sausage over medium heat until browned, breaking it up into pieces. Add garlic and cook for 1 minute.
    4. Stir in marinara sauce and simmer for 5 minutes. Remove from heat.

5. In a bowl, mix ricotta cheese, 1 cup mozzarella, Parmesan, egg, basil, oregano, salt, and pepper.

6. In a baking dish, layer pasta, ricotta mixture, sausage sauce, and the remaining mozzarella. Repeat layers, finishing with a layer of mozzarella.

7. Cover with foil and bake for 20 minutes. Remove foil and bake for an additional 10-15 minutes until cheese is bubbly and golden.

Beef Brisket

- Ingredients:

    1. 4-5 lb beef brisket
    2. 2 tbsp olive oil
    3. 1 onion, chopped
    4. 4 cloves garlic, minced
    5. 2 tbsp brown sugar
    6. 2 tbsp paprika
    7. 1 tbsp cumin
    8. 1 tbsp ground black pepper
    9. 1 tsp salt
    10. 1 cup beef broth
    11. 1/2 cup tomato paste

- Instructions:

    1. Preheat oven to 325°F (165°C).
    2. Rub brisket with olive oil and season with brown sugar, paprika, cumin, pepper, and salt.
    3. In a large oven-safe pot, heat olive oil over medium heat. Sear the brisket on both sides for 4-5 minutes until browned. Remove brisket and set aside.
    4. In the same pot, sauté onion and garlic for 5 minutes until softened.

5. Add beef broth and tomato paste, stirring to combine.

6. Return the brisket to the pot, cover with foil, and roast in the oven for 3-4 hours, or until tender.

7. Slice the brisket against the grain and serve with sauce from the pot.

Broccoli Cheddar Soup

- Ingredients:

    1. 2 tbsp butter
    2. 1 onion, chopped
    3. 2 cloves garlic, minced
    4. 4 cups broccoli florets
    5. 4 cups chicken broth
    6. 2 cups whole milk
    7. 2 cups shredded cheddar cheese
    8. 2 tbsp all-purpose flour
    9. Salt and pepper to taste

- Instructions:

    1. In a large pot, melt butter over medium heat. Sauté onion and garlic for 5 minutes until softened.
    2. Add broccoli and chicken broth, bringing it to a simmer. Cook for 10-12 minutes until broccoli is tender.
    3. In a separate bowl, whisk together flour and milk. Add this mixture to the soup, stirring constantly until it thickens, about 5 minutes.
    4. Stir in shredded cheddar cheese, salt, and pepper. Continue to cook until cheese is melted and the soup is smooth. Serve warm.

Chicken and Rice Casserole

- Ingredients:

    1. 2 cups cooked chicken, shredded
    2. 1 cup cooked rice
    3. 1 can (10.5 oz) cream of chicken soup
    4. 1 cup sour cream
    5. 1/2 cup shredded cheddar cheese
    6. 1/2 cup frozen peas (optional)
    7. 1/2 cup breadcrumbs
    8. 1 tbsp butter, melted

- Instructions:

    1. Preheat oven to 350°F (175°C).
    2. In a large bowl, combine chicken, rice, cream of chicken soup, sour cream, cheese, and peas. Mix well.
    3. Transfer to a greased casserole dish and spread evenly.
    4. In a small bowl, combine breadcrumbs and melted butter. Sprinkle over the top of the casserole.
    5. Bake for 25-30 minutes until the top is golden brown and the casserole is heated through.

Sausage and Peppers

- Ingredients:

    1. 4 Italian sausages
    2. 1 onion, sliced
    3. 2 bell peppers, sliced (red, yellow, or green)
    4. 2 tbsp olive oil
    5. 1 can (14.5 oz) diced tomatoes (optional)
    6. Salt and pepper to taste

- Instructions:

    1. Heat olive oil in a large skillet over medium heat. Add sausages and cook for 6-8 minutes per side until browned and cooked through.
    2. Remove sausages and set aside. In the same skillet, sauté onion and bell peppers for 5-7 minutes until softened.
    3. If using, add diced tomatoes and cook for an additional 5 minutes.
    4. Slice sausages and return to the skillet, stirring to combine with the peppers and onions. Serve hot.

Pot Roast with Carrots and Potatoes

- Ingredients:

    1. 3-4 lb beef chuck roast
    2. 4 cloves garlic, minced
    3. 2 tbsp olive oil
    4. 4 large carrots, peeled and cut into chunks
    5. 4 large potatoes, peeled and cut into chunks
    6. 2 cups beef broth
    7. 1 tbsp dried thyme
    8. 2 tbsp tomato paste
    9. Salt and pepper to taste

- Instructions:

    1. Preheat oven to 325°F (165°C).
    2. In a large Dutch oven, heat olive oil over medium-high heat. Brown the roast on all sides, about 4-5 minutes per side.
    3. Remove roast and set aside. Add garlic to the pot and sauté for 1 minute.
    4. Stir in tomato paste and beef broth, scraping up any browned bits from the bottom of the pot.
    5. Add carrots, potatoes, thyme, salt, and pepper. Return the roast to the pot.
    6. Cover and roast in the oven for 3-4 hours, or until the roast is tender and shreds easily.

Creamy Shrimp and Grits

- Ingredients:

    1. 1 lb shrimp, peeled and deveined
    2. 1 cup grits
    3. 4 cups water or chicken broth
    4. 1 cup heavy cream
    5. 2 tbsp butter
    6. 2 cloves garlic, minced
    7. 1/2 tsp smoked paprika
    8. 1/2 tsp cayenne pepper (optional)
    9. Salt and pepper to taste

- Instructions:

    1. Cook grits according to package directions, using water or broth. Stir in heavy cream, butter, salt, and pepper. Keep warm.
    2. In a skillet, melt butter over medium heat. Add garlic and sauté for 1 minute.
    3. Add shrimp, smoked paprika, cayenne pepper, salt, and pepper. Cook for 3-4 minutes until shrimp are pink and cooked through.
    4. Serve shrimp over grits and drizzle with any remaining sauce from the skillet.

Sautéed Garlic Spinach

- Ingredients:

    1. 4 cups fresh spinach

    2. 2 tbsp olive oil

    3. 4 cloves garlic, minced

    4. Salt and pepper to taste

- Instructions:

    1. Heat olive oil in a large skillet over medium heat. Add garlic and sauté for 1-2 minutes until fragrant.

    2. Add spinach and cook, stirring, until wilted, about 3-4 minutes.

    3. Season with salt and pepper and serve immediately.

Roasted Brussels Sprouts with Bacon

- Ingredients:

    1. 1 lb Brussels sprouts, trimmed and halved

    2. 4 slices bacon, chopped

    3. 2 tbsp olive oil

    4. Salt and pepper to taste

- Instructions:

    1. Preheat oven to 400°F (200°C).

    2. Toss Brussels sprouts with olive oil, salt, and pepper. Spread them on a baking sheet.

    3. Scatter chopped bacon over the Brussels sprouts.

    4. Roast for 20-25 minutes, stirring halfway through, until Brussels sprouts are crispy and browned and bacon is cooked.

Sweet Potato Casserole

- Ingredients:

    1. 4 large sweet potatoes, peeled and cubed
    2. 1/2 cup brown sugar
    3. 1/2 cup melted butter
    4. 1/4 cup milk
    5. 1 tsp cinnamon
    6. 1/2 tsp nutmeg
    7. 1/2 cup mini marshmallows (optional)

- Instructions:

    1. Preheat oven to 350°F (175°C).
    2. Boil sweet potatoes in a large pot of water until tender, about 15-20 minutes.
    3. Drain and mash the sweet potatoes with brown sugar, melted butter, milk, cinnamon, and nutmeg.
    4. Transfer to a baking dish and top with marshmallows, if desired.
    5. Bake for 20-25 minutes until heated through and marshmallows are golden.